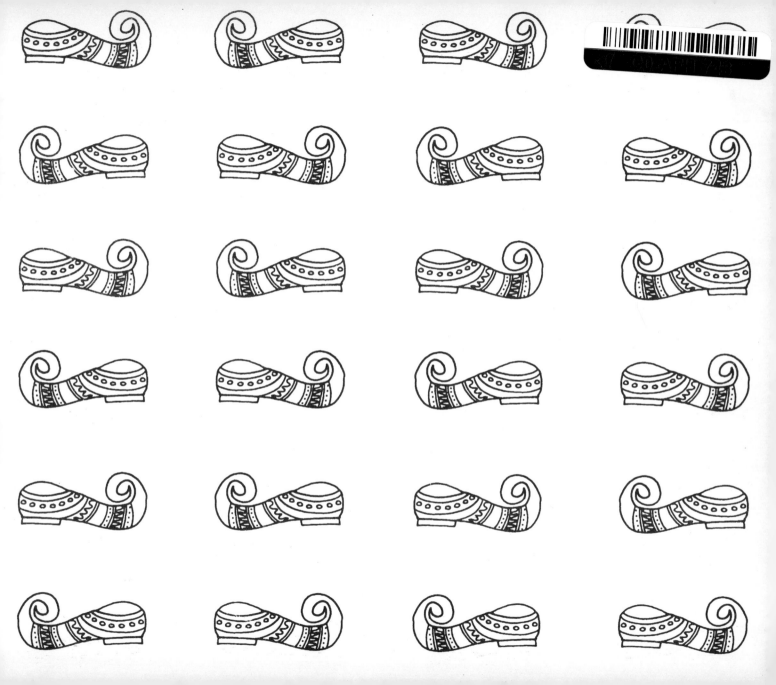

stories from india

under the banyan

Eyes on the Peacock's Tail a story from Rajasthan
Magic Vessels a story from Tamil Nadu
Hiss, Don't Bite! a story from Bengal
A Curly Tale a story from Bihar

Published by
Tulika Publishers, 7 Prithvi Avenue, Abhiramapuram, Chennai 600 018, India
email: kaka@tulikabooks.com
Visit our website at: http://www.tulikabooks.com

©1997 Vayu Naidu (text)
©1997 Tulika Publishers (illustrations)
First published in India, 1997

ISBN 81-86895-08-6

Distributed by
Goodbooks Marketing Pvt. Ltd., 7 Prithvi Avenue, Abhiramapuram,
Chennai 600 018, India

Printed and bound at
Anjan International Media, 27 J. J. Khan Road, Royapettah,
Chennai 600 014, India

Tulika

a folktale from bihar

A Curly Tale

by Vayu Naidu

art by Mugdha Shah

In Patna, the capital of Bihar, lived Kalia, a cobbler and his wife Swapan. They were famous for the special shoes they made. Shaped out of sturdy shining leather, the shoes curled in front with great style. All the rich and famous men of Patna — there were many in that prosperous city — wore Kalia's shoes.

"Squeak! Squeak!" went Lallubhai as he walked down the main road. Everybody stopped to watch him go by, his dhoti flapping in the wind.

"Squeak! Squeak! Squeak!" went Lakhanbhai as he sailed past, his shoes squeaking even louder. Everybody turned to watch him. Even Lallubhai.

It was said that the more powerful a man was, the louder his shoes squeaked. Wife, children and servants heard him coming from a great distance away. Quickly the children got off his favourite chair and the servant dusted it down.

Jadubhai, a very important man, had bought himself a pair of brand new shoes from Kalia. He couldn't wait to try them on. But first he sat on a charpai in his courtyard and puffed on his hookah. He sipped a glass of hot elaichi-flavoured tea. He sent Bhola the servant to fetch his betel-nut box. Then he put his feet into the new shoes.

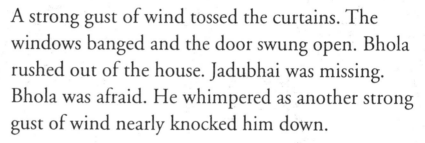

A strong gust of wind tossed the curtains. The windows banged and the door swung open. Bhola rushed out of the house. Jadubhai was missing. Bhola was afraid. He whimpered as another strong gust of wind nearly knocked him down.

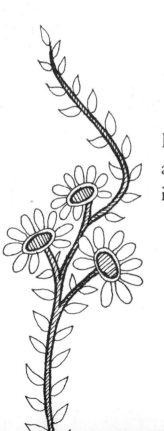

He watched with round eyes as a smokey blue mist appeared above the charpai. The tail of the mist seemed to disappear into a pair of brand new curly shoes.

Wait! They looked like Jadubhai's shoes. Oh! They sounded just like Jadubhai's shoes. Indeed, they were Jadubhai's shoes! Had his master become a bhoot, a g-g-g-ghost ? "Hai Ram!" moaned Bhola and fainted.

Kalia and Swapan lived on the other side of river Ganga where poor people from other trades lived.

"Funny isn't it?" Kalia said to Swapan one night as they were eating the last few grains of rice from a leaf bowl. "Funny how when people want their shoes they send their servants to our hut. They talk so sweetly to us because they want their job done."

"Hmm," said Swapan thoughtfully. "Funny, isn't it? When they have to pay us for the work we have done, they forget where we live. Forget even what we look like! They make us beg at their doors and then throw us only a small part of what they owe!"

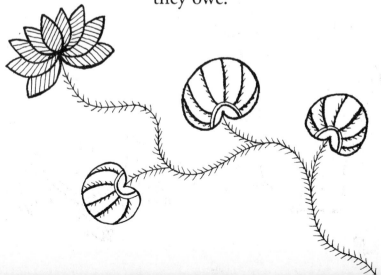

Kalia stood up. He picked up the hurricane lamp and raised its flame. The small room grew brighter and the shadows became smaller.

"I'm tired of being poor," he said. "Swapan, I'm going to do something about it right now."
"I'm going to do something about it right now!" imitated Swapan. "Huh! You've said this so many times before."
"This time I mean it," said Kalia.

Swapan only sighed loudly. She knew exactly what Kalia would do. Kalia tied a cloth round his head and hurried out of the hut. The hurricane lamp bounced up and down in the huge darkness and the light shone dim. But at least Kalia could see where he was going.

Kalia reached a grove of sal trees. He saw a small red light piercing the black night. He walked towards it. The smell of tobacco grew strong. Leaning against a tree sat a man with long matted hair. He wore beads around his neck. The light that Kalia saw was the burning end of his beedi.

Kalia knelt in front of the man. "Oh holy one," he cried, "only you can help me. Please, please find me a ghost who can make me some money! I am sick and tired of being poor."

"Hmmm," replied the holy man. "Are you sure this is what you want?" "Oh yes!" replied Kalia. "Okay then. Areyoooo!" the holy man called, snapping his fingers three times.

There was a swish of smokey blue mist and a ghost stood beside him. The ghost wore a pair of curly shoes. "But this is Jadubhai!" exclaimed Kalia, recognising the shoes.
Yes indeed, it was the missing Jadubhai!

"So," grunted the ghost, "I am Bhootram,
your servant. What can I do for you?"

"B-b-baap re!" gulped Kalia. The ghost's voice sent
shivers down his spine. It didn't seem such a good
idea after all. But he swallowed his fear and said,
"Bhootramji, I-I-I want money. Lots of money. But
no cheating, hanh!"

"Awwwlrrright!" replied Bhootram with a flourish.
"Give me some work to do and I will earn money
for you. But remember, you have to keep giving me
work or else I will eat you up, and your wife too!"
He looked like he meant it.

Kalia thought for a moment and said, "It is
time to plant the mahua seeds from here
where the sun rises to there where it sets."

Bhootram pulled out a bag of gold coins from
nowhere and gave it to Kalia. "Here you are, Kaliaji.
Here's the money that will come out of this job."
And he took off in a cloud of smoke and dust.

"Aiii! So much money!" exclaimed Kalia. He was surprised and a little afraid. "Well, this will last us for the next three months by which time Bhootram would have finished planting the seeds." He ran home to Swapan.

Next morning, Swapan awoke with a start. "What is that noise?" she asked Kalia. It sounded like the clatter of vessels. There stood Bhootram, a pot in each hand, ready to throw them. Swapan shrieked.

"Where is Kalia? I've finished the sowing," Bhootram snarled. "Give me something else to do or else I will..." Bhootram made a chomping sound. Kalia shivered.

"Okay! Okay! No need to make us jump," said Swapan firmly. "Harvest the mahua crop, all two thousand acres of it, brew it into wine and keep it ready for the Holi festivities." Bhootram pulled out many many bags of gold and threw them on the floor and once more rushed off to do his job.

"What a scared crow you are!" Swapan said to Kalia, who, by now, was quaking with fear. "By the time the seeds sprout and the trees grow and the mahua blossoms are harvested, it will be many months." "Don't be too sure," warned Kalia.

Sure enough by mid-day it seemed as though the season itself had changed. And indeed it had. The mahua trees were beginning to flower. In a little while Bhootram returned. The wine was ready to drink.

"Oh my god!" said Kalia. "He'll surely eat us now. I had better do something." Kalia raced off towards the sal grove. Bhootram came chasing after him as he stumbled over stones and crashed through bushes. He reached the sal grove and flung himself at the holy man's feet.

"Sir! Sir! Help! This ghost is too much for me. He's even moved the seasons forward. I can't think of any more work to give him. What shall I do?" Bhootram stood huffing and puffing behind Kalia.

The holy man looked at Bhootram.
At that moment a puppy-dog came by. He had a tail as curly as an onion ring.
"Hurry up!" growled Bhootram. "Give me something to do or else…" He was really angry now.

Kalia and the holy man looked at the puppy. They looked at each other. They nodded. "Okay Bhootram," said Kalia, "see this puppy here? Catch hold of him and straighten his tail."
"You have made me wait so long," complained Bhootram and ran behind the puppy. "Oh, I almost forgot," he said, and flung bags of gold at Kalia.

Bhootram picked up the puppy and sat under Banyan. Zoing! he pulled out its tail. But the moment he let go, Boing! it curled up again. Again he tried Zoing! Again it went Boing! Zoing! Boing! Zoing! Boing!

Hours, days, weeks, months sped by. Banyan's aerial roots began to touch the ground. The puppy grew into a dog. But its curly tail refused to become straight.

Many years later there was a knock on Kalia's door. He and
Swapan now lived in a small house. In fact, all the people on
their side of the river now lived in sweet, small houses.
There were trees and flowers and birds.

Swapan opened the door. Kalia stood behind her.
Bhootram stood there in a smokey blue mist quite
grey with despair. He was sobbing. At his heel stood
the dog with the curly tail.

"Kaliaji, Swapanji, please keep this dog and everything I have
given you. I promise never to ask for any more work. This
dog's tail can never be straightened. I want to go home, back
to my sal trees," Bhootram cried.

"Certainly," said Kalia. "And thank you for all you have
given us and our friends." He went to the holy man in the
sal grove and told him he didn't need a ghost any more.
The holy man smiled and with a whoosh Bhootram returned
to his safe and secret home.

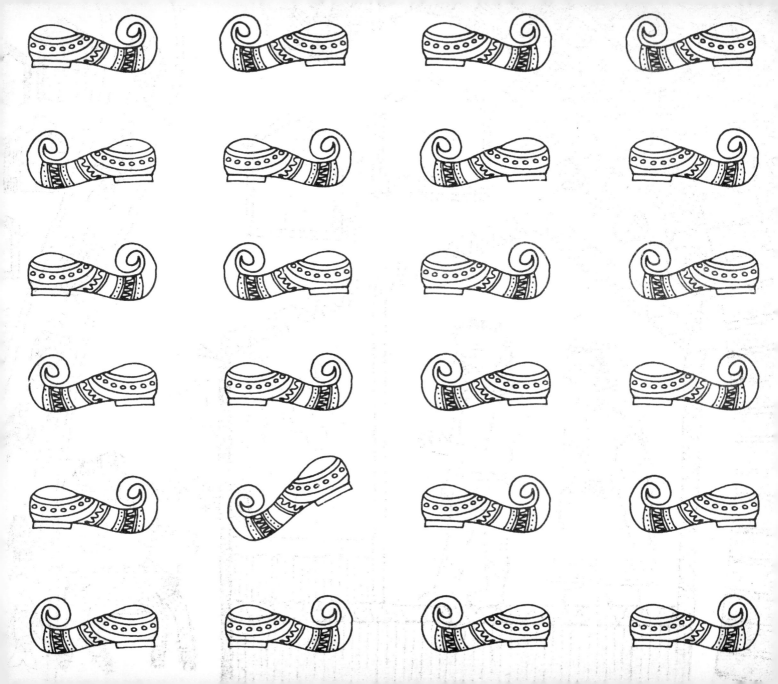